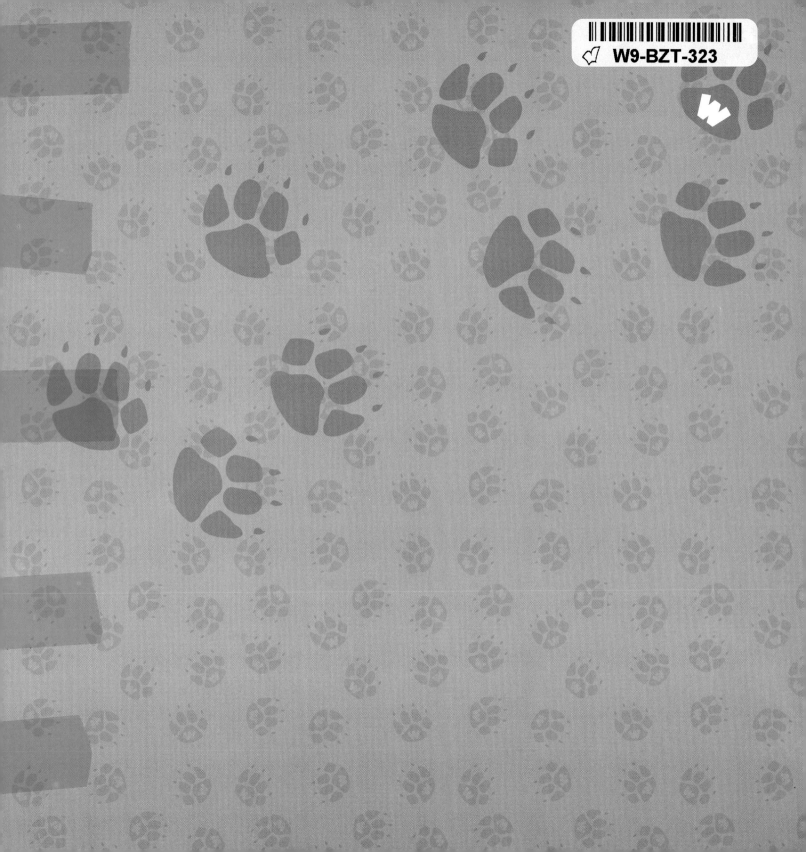

To my new nephew, Dylan Louie.
Another one of the world's cutest creatures.

What Is Mr. Winkle?

Lara Jo Regan

Random House  New York

What is Mr. Winkle?

Mr. Winkle entered my life in a manner as improbable and mystical as he is. Lost in an industrial area on my way home from a photography assignment, I spotted an odd tuft of fluff on the side of the road. Moving close enough to take in its diminutive dimensions and enormous, otherworldly eyes, I thought it might be a shipwrecked alien. In the glow of the headlights, this muddy, tattered little creature hobbled straight into my arms, as if he'd been waiting for me all along.

After a year of vet visits and tender loving care, my peculiar pint-sized pal was well enough to lead a normal life. It took even longer to come up with a name worthy of his uniqueness. Finally, it came to me—Mr. Winkle! Of course.

As his health improved, Mr. Winkle began to meet people on his daily walks, all of whom offered theories as to his identity. "It's a robotic squirrel!" screamed a cable repairman. "It's a cat in a dog suit," surmised an out-of-work actor. "He's a furry smile!" exclaimed a Japanese tourist.

It was these hilarious, inspired reactions from mesmerized strangers that sparked the idea for the *What Is Mr. Winkle?* photo series. His power to heal, enchant, and entertain was too overwhelming to keep to myself. I simply had to share him with the world through my photography. Mr. Winkle made it easy, supermodel that he turned out to be. He loves the camera, hamming it up with all his heart, as if he knows it's his mission to make us happy.

What is Mr. Winkle? Well, that's for you to decide. I'm sure you will choose a favorite character or two. Mine is one I haven't made a photo of yet, but I think it may be what Mr. Winkle *truly* is: the child of a cloud, on loan from heaven.

—Lara Jo Regan

A Bumblebear?

A Ghost?

A Thirsty Camel?

An Ancient Koala?

A Hamster with a Perm?

A Japanese Cartoon Character?

A BEDROOM SLIPPER?

a stuffed animal?

A Cat in a Dog Suit?

A Marionette?

A Wood Sprite?

A Bowwow Ballerina?

A Dashboard Ornament?

AN ALIEN?

A Devil?

What *Is* Mr. Winkle?

The cutest dog in the universe!

(A Pom-pom?)

Published in the United States by Random House, Inc., New York, and simultaneously in Canada by Random House of Canada Limited, Toronto.
www.randomhouse.com/kids
www.mrwinkle.com
Library of Congress Control Number: 2001089275
ISBN: 0-375-81554-6
Printed in the United States of America October 2001 10 9 8 7 6 5 4 3 2
RANDOM HOUSE and colophon are registered trademarks of Random House, Inc.